P9-CCX-735

Holidays—Count and Celebrate!

Martin Luther King, Jr., Day

Count and Celebrate!

Fredrick L. McKissack, Jr. and Lisa Beringer McKissack

Enslow Elementary

an imprint of

 Enslow Publishers, Inc.

40 Industrial Road
Box 398
Berkeley Heights, NJ 07922
USA

http://www.enslow.com

*To our parents and grandparents who followed Dr. King
so we, too, could live the dream.*

Enslow Elementary, an imprint of Enslow Publishers, Inc.

Enslow Elementary® is a registered trademark of Enslow Publishers, Inc.

Copyright © 2009 by Enslow Publishers, Inc.

Library of Congress Cataloging-in-Publication Data

McKissack, Fredrick, Jr.
    Martin Luther King, Jr., Day—count and celebrate! / Fredrick L. McKissack, Jr. and Lisa Beringer McKissack.
        p. cm. — (Holidays-count and celebrate!)
    Includes bibliographical references and index.
    Summary: "Kids count from one to ten as they learn about the history of Martin Luther King, Jr., Day"—Provided by publisher.
    ISBN-13: 978-0-7660-3105-0
    1. Martin Luther King, Jr., Day—Juvenile literature. 2. King, Martin Luther, Jr., 1929–1968—Juvenile literature. 3. Counting—Juvenile literature.
I. McKissack, Lisa Beringer. II. Title.
    E185.97.K5M359 2009
    394.261—dc22   2007046811

ISBN-10: 0-7660-3105-5

Printed in the United States of America

10 9 8 7 6 5 4 3 2 1

To Our Readers: We have done our best to make sure all Internet Addresses in this book were active and appropriate when we went to press. However, the author and the publisher have no control over and assume no liability for the material available on those Internet sites or on other Web sites they may link to. Any comments or suggestions can be sent by e-mail to comments@enslow.com or to the address on the back cover.

Every effort has been made to locate all copyright holders of material used in this book. If any errors or omissions have occurred, corrections will be made in future editions of this book.

♻ Enslow Publishers, Inc., is committed to printing our books on recycled paper. The paper in every book contains 10% to 30% post-consumer waste (PCW). The cover board on the outside of each book contains 100% PCW. Our goal is to do our part to help young people and the environment too!

Illustration Credits: A Posh Sentinel Productions, pp. 2, 13; Associated Press, pp. 5, 7, 9 (both), 11, 13, 15, 17, 21, 25, 28 (numbers 1, 2, 3, 4, 5), 29 (numbers 6, 8, 10); © 2008 Jupiterimages Corporation, pp. 2, 30; PhotoEdit, Inc., 19, 29 (number 7); Shutterstock, p. 27; Jim West/The Image Works, pp. 23, 29 (number 9).

Cover Illustration: Associated Press

Contents

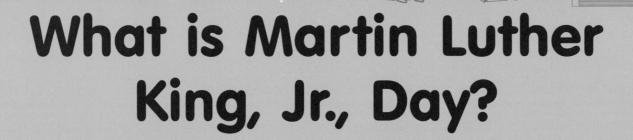

What is Martin Luther King, Jr., Day?

Martin Luther King, Jr., Day is a special holiday to remember the life of Dr. Martin Luther King, Jr. He was a great civil rights leader. A civil rights leader is someone who helps people when they are not treated well. We celebrate Dr. King's life on the third Monday in January. This day is very close to his birthday. He was born on January 15, 1929.

activist (AK-tih-vist)—Someone who works to make the world a better place.

civil rights—The freedoms that belong to all people.

civil rights movement—A group of people who work to get civil rights for everyone.

equality (e-KWAL-I-tee)—When people are treated the same.

nonviolence (non-VY-eh-lints)—Not using force or fighting.

peace—A time when there is no war or violence.

unity (YOU-nuh-tee)—Working together as part of a group.

How many Nobel Peace Prizes were given to Martin Luther King, Jr.?

One

Dr. Martin Luther King, Jr., spent his life working to help people live in peace. On December 10, 1964, he was awarded **one** Nobel Peace Prize. This is a very special prize given to people who work for peace. Dr. King was the youngest person ever to be given this award. He believed people could love one another and live together without fear and hate. On Martin Luther King, Jr., Day, people work to make the world a better and more peaceful place for others.

1

7

1

How many presidents did Martin Luther King, Jr., meet?

Two

Dr. Martin Luther King, Jr., met with **two** American presidents. They were John F. Kennedy and Lyndon B. Johnson. He asked them to help pass a law that would give all people equal rights. He also talked about a big event that was going to take place in Washington, D.C., the capital of the United States. This was called the March on Washington. It was very important. It let people know that Dr. King was not alone in trying to get civil rights. People from all over the country came together to march on Washington in 1963.

John F.
Kennedy

Lyndon B.
Johnson

Martin
Luther
King, Jr.

Martin
Luther
King, Jr.

1

2

How many kids are holding a banner in a parade?
Three

Many people march in parades on Martin Luther King, Jr., Day. Taking part in parades reminds people we need to keep working for peace and civil rights. These **three** kids are holding a banner as they march in a parade.

How many girls make a special quilt?

Four

These **four** girls are making a quilt (KWILT). Each square shows a different hero. A square may also show what being a hero means to someone. Many people think of Dr. Martin Luther King, Jr., as a hero. He helped people get civil rights. It was not an easy job. Some people did not like his ideas and tried to stop him. They had him put in jail. They even said they would hurt him and his family. But Dr. King is a hero to many people because he did not give up his work. He kept fighting for freedom and equality—no matter the danger.

This is what a hero quilt square may look like.

I HAVE A DREAM

How many people are in this family photo?
Five

This picture shows **five** people in Dr. Martin Luther King, Jr.'s, family. There is Dr. King; his wife, Coretta Scott King; and three of his four children, Yolanda, Martin Luther King III, and Dexter. Dr. King has one other daughter, Bernice.

Like her husband, Coretta Scott King was a civil rights activist. After Dr. King died, Mrs. King started the King Center to teach nonviolence. The King Center helps people learn how to make the world a better place.

How many leaders are in this photograph?
Six

The **six** men in this photo worked together to create the March on Washington in 1963. All of these men were civil rights leaders. Whitney Young, Jr., and Roy Wilkins were leaders in civil rights groups that worked with presidents of the United States to bring about equal rights. A. Philip Randolph wanted people to be treated fairly at their jobs. John Lewis was a member of a student group that wanted freedom for all people. James Farmer, Jr., started a group that worked to make buses open to all people. For many years, African Americans could not ride buses with white people.

1 John Lewis

2 Whitney Young, Jr.

3 A. Philip Randolph

4 Martin Luther King, Jr.

5 James Farmer, Jr.

6 Roy Wilkins

How many kids help plant a garden?
Seven

These **seven** kids help plant a garden during their day of volunteering. Many people spend Martin Luther King, Jr., Day helping others. Some people paint houses. Others collect canned food for the poor. Some volunteers read to kids, while others spend time with older people. Whatever they do, Martin Luther King, Jr., Day is a day to help others.

1

How many flags do you see?

Eight

On Martin Luther King, Jr., Day people all over the United States march in parades. The **eight** kids in this picture are holding flags. Martin Luther King, Jr., Day is a time to celebrate Dr. King's life with flags, music, and dancing. These things show how thankful people are for Dr. King's work.

How many kids march during a Martin Luther King, Jr., Day parade?

Nine

These **nine** kids are marching in a parade and holding signs. Martin Luther King, Jr., Day is a day of helping other people. There are a lot of ways kids can take part in making a difference. Kids can volunteer to help others. They can march in a parade. They can collect food and clothing for homeless shelters. Helping others does not have to be hard. Kids can find ways to help at their school or in their neighborhood.

How many buttons are on this jacket?
Ten

People can show their support for civil rights in many different ways. This person is wearing **ten** Dr. Martin Luther King, Jr., buttons on her coat. Wearing buttons keeps the life and work of Dr. King in people's thoughts all year. We do not have to wait for Martin Luther King, Jr., Day to work for civil rights. Every day people can make the world a better place by volunteering and working for equality and peace.

deserved to be treated fairly under the law. Sadly, he was killed for what he believed. He died on April 4, 1968, in Memphis, Tennessee. He was just thirty-nine years old. Within days of Dr. King's death, people began asking for a holiday to remember him—and to continue his work for peace and equality.

Today, Martin Luther King, Jr., Day is celebrated by people in the United States and in other places around the world. People are asked to make it "a day on, not a day off." People volunteer, attend church services, and talk about issues like equal rights for all people. In some places, people hold parades or go to churches to hear people speak about Dr. King and his life. Martin Luther King, Jr., believed that all people, regardless of the color of their skin, should work for peace and equality. On Martin Luther King, Jr., Day, people make that dream a reality.

Count Again!

1		One
2		Two
3		Three
4		Four
5		Five

MARTIN LUTHER KING, Jr. DAY

Count Again!

6		Six
7		Seven
8		Eight
9		Nine
10		Ten

Words to Know

boycott—To stop using something in order to make a point.

law—A rule that is to be followed.

march—A gathering of people who walk together for a special purpose.

minister—The leader of a church.

speech—A talk given to a large group of people.

volunteer—Someone who spends time helping others.

Learn More

Books

Myers, Walter Dean. *I've Seen the Promised Land: The Life of Dr. Martin Luther King, Jr.* New York: HarperCollins Publishers, 2004.

Nobleman, Marc Tyler. *Martin Luther King Jr. Day.* Minneapolis, Minn.: Compass Point Books, 2005.

Trueit, Trudi Strain. *Martin Luther King Jr. Day.* New York: Children's Press, 2006.

Internet Addresses

The King Center
<http://www.thekingcenter.org/index.asp>

Martin Luther King Jr. and the Civil Rights Movement
<http://seattletimes.nwsource.com/special/mlk/>

Index